The
Touring
Caravan
Story

T0346775

The
Touring
Caravan
Story

Over a Century of Towing

Andrew Jenkinson

The
History
Press

Andrew Jenkinson has written multiple books on the history of touring caravans, static caravans and motorhomes, and he writes for *Practical Caravan*, *Practical Motorhome* and *Park Home Holiday Living* magazines. He also contributes to the Caravan and Motorhome Club and the Camping and Caravanning Club, and has appeared on both TV and radio. As well as gathering a vast archive, he tests both new and used tourers, motorhomes and holiday caravans and hosts a popular YouTube channel. He lives on the outskirts of Blackpool in Lancashire.

First published 2022

The History Press
97 St George's Place, Cheltenham,
Gloucestershire, GL50 3QB
www.thehistorypress.co.uk

British Library Cataloguing in Publication Data.
A catalogue record for this book is available from the British Library.

ISBN 978 0 7509 9491 0

Typesetting and origination by The History Press
Printed in Turkey by Imak

Contents

Foreword

My interest in the touring caravan grew from an early age. My grandparents had a tourer from the late 1950s, as did my parents from 1969, and I had one myself from 1985. The growth of caravanning exploded into a boom time by the late 1960s. With more affluent lifestyles and increased car ownership, the touring caravan was seen as an instant ideal way to get away from it all. This book is about the car-pulled caravan from its humble beginnings as a rich man's interest to the holiday of choice for the everyday family. It contains history and also memories from those who have caravanned over the years. It also considers the folding caravan and looks at how this was to become a choice for some. This isn't a complete history of all the manufacturers – space wouldn't permit! – but if you are new to caravanning, I hope this book will give you an insight into how it has evolved over 100 years.

With some of my own personal happy memories included as well, this book explains how folk caravanned and what they used to do so both car-wise and in terms of accessories. It's a nostalgic look at the touring caravan from 1919 to the present day – a story that has many twists and turns as sales boomed and slumped. As I write this book, caravanning has seen a massive surge in the UK and the rest of Europe, but it has all been seen before and, with new electric cars seeing their own boom, the touring caravan is set to see further changes. But for now, sit back and enjoy the world of the caravanner through the decades.

Andrew Jenkinson

1.

1919 – A Rich Man's Pastime

The story of the touring caravan as we know it today stretches back to the late 1800s. A certain Dr Gordon Stables, a well-travelled retired naval officer, wrote a number of boys' adventure stories based on his experiences. Stables also decided to travel around the UK, camping and writing of his adventures along the way, and he witnessed Gypsies who travelled with their own homes: horse-drawn caravans. Stables noted how these caravans were built in a certain style. Fascinated by this way of life, Stables looked more deeply into the lifestyle of freedom these go-anywhere folk enjoyed.

Dr Gordon Stables was the pioneer of using a caravan for leisure, writing several books such as this in the late 1800s.

Stables didn't want a 'real Gypsy caravan'; he basically wanted a flat on wheels and his design was very luxurious.

Stables wanted one of these horse-drawn caravans and decided to have one built for him by the Bristol Wagon Co. His caravan was aptly named *The Wanderer*, and in it he began to travel with his assistant, who slept underneath. Stables began writing about his travels in *The Wanderer* and the folk he met on the way. Unknowingly, Stables had in fact become the founder of the leisure caravan movement.

Stables travelled in style, oh yes! He wanted to portray the life of a Gypsy, but he saw himself as a gentleman, after all, and wanted to be treated as such. With his valet and horseman plus his dog Hurricane Bob and a parrot named Polly, Stables was, in modern terms, an eccentric. His books sold well and he made a nice income waxing lyrical about his adventures. He also told it like it was when an industrial town was on his route,

The early 1900s saw horse-drawn caravanning become a hit with the rich and they often took servants with them who slept in tents.

writing about children with no shoes and ragged clothes. No doubt he hid away in *The Wanderer* until the scenery changed.

Fun fact: Horse-drawn caravanners were often mistaken for Gypsies!

The important part of this – our story of the touring caravan – is how Stables' exploits in his luxury flat on wheels began to inspire others. The Duke of Newcastle took the plunge and had the Bristol Wagon Co. build him his own caravan, at a cost of £450, that he named *The Bohemian*. It was equipped with a large stove and wine cellar! As with Stables, many people mistook the duke for a showman, a Gypsy or a hawker of goods. But both men always put folk firmly in their place as to who they were. The spread of the 'Gentleman Gypsy' idea saw the rich also decide to take up this type of holiday so they too could boast to their friends of the many adventures they had in their caravan.

Stables preached about health, happiness and good clean air. In his book of 1886, *The Cruise of the Land Yacht Wanderer*, he described his caravan in great detail and this inspired more 'Gentleman Gypsies'. Other books were written and a small movement surrounding leisure caravans began to emerge. In 1907, J. Harris Stone held a meeting at his home with other like-minded folk and formed the Caravan Club of Great Britain.

The age of caravanning had begun and, with the petrol engine becoming more reliable, some people considered adapting small trucks with living accommodation added as one-off motorised caravans. Harris Stone wasn't keen on the idea but was soon impressed by several new members' motorised caravans. During the First World War, the horse-drawn caravan owner struggled as horses were taken for the armed forces, leaving many caravans without pulling power, and this increased the use of cars as tugs.

In 1901, Mr Holding, a keen cyclist and camper, convinced others that camping was

Formed in 1901, the Camping Club allowed in caravanners, including those with horse-pulled, motorised and car-pulled types.

possible on cycle trips using new lightweight camping gear. He and the Rev. E.C. Pitt-Johnson, an undergraduate at New College, Oxford, formed the Association of Cycle Campers, which began to attract new members. By 1906 this had become the Camping Club, which allowed the horse-drawn caravan owner to join. The new trailer caravan and motorised caravan was also allowed in under the club's new name, the Camping and Caravan Club.

Fast forward to 1918–19, after the First World War, and the car would prove a solution for the new modern leisure caravanner as reliability was improved along with engine power. However, these car-pulled caravans could not be as heavy or as large as the horse-drawn type. In 1919, a father-and-son team in Birmingham saw the future of caravanning with cars, although designing such vehicles was not easy. The men, both named Bill Riley, had experimented with a motor caravan conversion pre-war.

Riley Junior had towed trailers in the conflict and convinced his father to go ahead with a

A rare clear image of the Rileys' Eccles first trailer car-pulled caravan in 1919. It was the beginning of the modern tourer of today.

An early Eccles chassis design – the Rileys were ahead of the game with their innovative ideas.

trailer caravan, so the pair worked hard designing a primitive version. They sold their transport business but kept the name Eccles and began making trailer and motor caravans, although convincing buyers was difficult. Construction was in aluminium and wood, with some early makers using wood for the chassis; this idea was soon dropped for steel, with Eccles leading in chassis design.

Eccles' interiors would become noted for craftsmanship and layouts that were practical while still using the rear door entry. However, Car

The Eccles interiors were high in quality for the time and also had well-thought-out, practical designs.

Cruiser would put entrance doors on the side and design a different layout. The early 1920s caravans soon developed their own look, with their only resemblance to the horse-drawn design being the 'Molly Croft roof' or lantern roof, as it became known; only more expensive models used this design due to the work involved and extra expense.

> **Fun fact:** Early caravanners often carried a pistol in case of attempted theft from their caravan!

Coverage in various newspapers helped caravan sales but again only the rich could afford them. The Rileys began the first commercial caravan manufacturing facility at their Gosta Green works in Birmingham. Meanwhile, Bertram Hutchings had hired horse-drawn caravans that he had designed and built pre-war, but he also saw the Rileys' efforts and set about designing car-pulled trailer caravans. Hiring was

Bertram Hutchings was an early builder of horse-drawn models.

Why Not a Caravanning Holiday?

An Experiment which Motorists Can Make upon Hiring a Caravan Equipment.

GIVEN fine weather, there are few ways of enjoying a holiday that can better a tour with a car and trailer caravan, for, if desired, one can have a different camp every day, in addition to the fact that one is entirely independent of hotels, if desired, electric light may be had as an extra. When the hire of a trailer is contemplated it is well to inform the concern as to the horse-power and type of car it is proposed to use, for their recommendations as to the most suitable type of

Three picturesque caravan sites.   (Left) On the banks of Loch Lomond.   (Centre and right) In the heart of the Cotswolds.

The national press was keen to report on this new 'caravanning' idea, with articles published on a regular basis.

17

a good way to make sales as many new dealers hired out caravans and the hirer would then usually buy them.

Primitive designs involved 2.5m-long models sleeping two, but by the early 1920s progress was being made quite swiftly. The motorised caravanner was a new breed compared with those who owned horse-drawn vehicles, which were now seen as behind the times. These new motorised caravanners were keen to explore the UK and would set off and potter down the byways, stopping off at idyllic pitches. These were often by a river, where they could camp, usually with a separate tent for visitors. Even newly-weds would hire a caravan for a honeymoon in the great outdoors.

Left: By the late 1920s the horse-drawn caravan was seen as old fashioned – the car-pulled type was to prevail.

Opposite: Many early caravanners would stop in a secluded spot and make camp.

A CARAVAN HONEYMOON

I.—Pages from the Log of the Good Ship "Carrie," Bound to the West Country with a Crew of Two (Not Forgetting the Dog).

by

L. W. A. BAILY.

It seemed that everybody wanted to try the caravanning lark — even newly-weds, who wrote of their experiences on the road.

One couple wrote several articles for *Autocar* in 1928 about their caravanning honeymoon, during which they took their dog on a three-week UK tour. Towing a hired Eccles De-Luxe caravan behind a two-seater Morris Cowley, the couple wrote of their adventures and the joy of caravan camping. Their account would encourage others to take up the hobby but mainly on a hiring basis. The couple also told of the pitfalls, such as pitching on soft ground, as well as the need to tow at a good steady speed of just 20mph! They also wrote of how they could stop in a village or town and a crowd of folk would gaze through the windows. The sight of a car-pulled caravan was a novelty to many, which is hard to believe today!

Lord Baden Powell, who had a loyal following and had founded the Scout movement, would himself become a caravan owner. In 1929 he was presented with an Eccles at a jamboree and after his death it was in need of some light restoration. The Eccles was sent back to the factory to be ready for the Sutton Coldfield 1957 jamboree. Incidentally, the caravan is still around and some years ago was exhibited at the NEC Caravan and Motorhome Show in all its glory!

Fun fact: The horse-drawn caravanner often sent a servant ahead on a bike to check villages for supplies.

Bill Riley with the Lord Baden Powell caravan at the Eccles works in 1957 after restoration.

The press picked up on the growing movement, publishing letters from these new leisure seekers who could tow their accommodation behind them. New firms and new designs cropped up as sales grew. No sites were established specifically for caravans, only for tents, but some farmers would allow several caravans in a field they owned for a small fee. These became established by word of mouth, as often in the early 1920s one owner would stop to chat to another caravanner. However, many of the new caravanners just wanted to stop as and where they wanted down small lanes in a lay-by or on a beach.

Left: The motoring press also suggested the caravan as an ideal way to explore the UK in the late 1920s.

Opposite: Early 1920s caravan pitched up in a field. Farmers often found a place for this new leisure seeker.

Some would hire a caravan for several weeks. A favourite spot was the beach, with access back then being easier than it is today.

Opposite: These types of caravans that dropped down over the lower section for towing were hard to operate in damp weather as wood expanded!

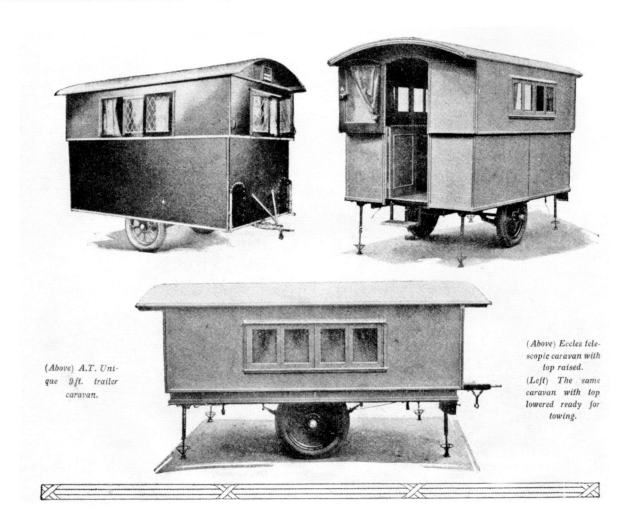

(*Above*) A.T. Uni-
que 9 ft. trailer
caravan.

(*Above*) Eccles tele-
scopic caravan with
top raised.
(*Left*) The same
caravan with top
lowered ready for
towing.

Back then many villages and indeed towns remained isolated, with little contact with the outside world. The car had opened up new opportunities for folk to explore, but the caravan now meant a month's touring in comfort was perfectly possible. However, some people did not want to tow such a caravan and early small makers tried out new ideas to try to fill this gap. In the early 1920s the collapsible caravan was seen as a way forward for those who found it too daunting to tow a caravan. Unfortunately, in damp weather the wood expanded and the caravan was difficult to collapse down.

The Trek was a take on a tent trailer but was considered to be a caravan. It was easy to tow.

Shadow collapsible caravans proved quite successful in the late 1920s.

The ideal holiday.

Patents Pending.

Other ideas were tried, such as where the top half of the caravan slid over the bottom half for towing, but they were not successful. Then there was an early trailer-tent-type caravan by Trek, a small company in the mid-1920s, which had a canvas pull-up roof. It was basic and was designed to appeal to the camper who wanted a caravan but still have the feel of a tent. Shadow caravans of Wolverhampton would capture some of this niche market with their designs.

Fun fact: Caravans were rare in the 1920s and, if one stopped in a village, a crowd would usually gather with their faces pressed against the windows looking in!

Opposite: Once pitched, it was assembled for use. Dad smokes as he watches the kettle for a brew.

Motor Caravans and Trailers for all Climates.

12-ft. Eccles De Luxe Trailer Caravan.

Specially built to withstand tropical heat.

Supplied by us to His Highness The Rajah of Kalsia.

ECCLES LONDON DEPOT : THE P. & P. MOTOR CO.,
132-140, MARKHOUSE ROAD, WALTHAMSTOW, LONDON, E.17.
London Agents and Distributors for Essex, Hertfordshire, Bedfordshire and Cambridgeshire.

Page FOURTEEN

Right: By the late 1920s Eccles were selling adapted UK models to far-off countries.

An Eccles leaves the factory in a large crate for export to Bombay, India.

The caravanning idea was spreading and royalty from various countries purchased these homes on wheels. Eccles, the true pioneers of the touring caravan, found orders coming in for larger caravans, wanted for hunting-trip accommodation. A good number of Eccles were exported globally, with Indian royalty especially attracted to the designs and ornate craftsmanship. Eccles developed new ideas and designs, as did their competitors, such as Raven, Winchester, Car Cruiser and Summerfield (later renamed Cheltenham).

Only the better off could buy or even hire a caravan back then, and only when prices dropped would ownership grow. Slowly an accessory market began to evolve around the new caravanning idea, including lean-to tents

A wireless set adds to the pleasures of a caravan holiday. We are pleased to advise as to suitable sets and to supply our customers.

The lean-to tent or awning was a new accessory, plus a new portable radio would provide entertainment in your van.

An Appreciation.

GRANADA, SPAIN.

November 17th, 1929.

Dear Sir,

Your Caravan has been quite too marvellous.

I left Dieppe with it on Nov. 5th and arrived here Nov. 15th. coming through the middle of Spain over the most awful roads, in some places where they were being repaired.

I came in for a terrific thunderstorm in the mountains beyond St. Sebastian, I thought the rain would have broken the roof.

It is a marvellously made Caravan and has stood the journey in a miraculous way.

I cannot say too much in its praise.

Please use this letter if of any use,

Yours faithfully,

Signed   E. K. HARDY.

(awnings), loo tents, lamps, stoves and even a travel radio set for entertainment. The original leather hitch loop coupling on a caravan was soon replaced by a steel pin coupling, although adding a towing bracket to a car was still a job for an engineer or blacksmith!

The Raven caravan of the late 1920s looked like a rail goods wagon in style! Owners wrote of the high quality and design.

TOURING HOLIDAY ON THE GROUND FLOOR

Business girls from Bristol find a spot in the sun while on a caravan tour in Somerset.

PR was always good for the new caravan movement, with posed shots like this using young women as models.

Car Cruiser had been building streamlined caravans from the early 1920s. The door is on the side, a fashion that other makers followed.

"Caravanning"

THE IDEAL HOLIDAY

THE ONLY WAY

AN Eccles Trailer Caravan is the only way to ensure a holiday of complete freedom, with all the comfort demanded these days, and with more than usual economy. No roughing it—just a mobile home with all the necessities for a holiday of three weeks or three months.

Our Service does not end with the supply of a caravan—we satisfy every need of the motor caravanner, including such details as camp site addresses in any part of the country.

"Caravanning," the Handbook of the Ideal Holiday, will give you full particulars. Write for a copy now —or call and inspect.

WL 4600

The Holiday Caravan Co. Ltd
Bainton Rd. Oxford

Hiring proved lucrative, with the Holiday Caravan Co. doing well using Eccles models. Many hirers bought a caravan after a holiday in one.

Owners sent testimonials about how well their Eccles or Raven caravan had performed in various tours around the world. It was all good publicity for the brands, but also for the fledgling caravan trade. With caravans costing around £100 plus, it would be a few years before prices would be affordable, but as new suppliers came to the industry, the price of components became cheaper. The coverage being given to caravanning also promoted the attractions of visiting the great outdoors.

Fun fact: Essential equipment included a spade for digging a loo – and the user was asked to replace the turf afterwards!

The original square designs that leant to the horse-drawn era gradually gave way to more streamlined models. Small dealers were set up and these mainly hired caravans on a seasonal basis. With no gas or insulation, the 1920s caravans were limited to use in summer.

Several hire companies did become quite large, such as the Holiday Caravan Company based in Oxford, which offered Eccles models.

The season began in April, but that didn't stop the early caravanners setting off on a snowy Easter break. The Eccles brand was being noticed by the press, which would feature caravan holiday articles. The old horse-drawn caravan was still being used, and many caravanners would hire a horse for 30s a week, including attendant.

The 1920s saw Eccles in the lead in design and layout, while firms such as the fledgling Car Cruiser went for early streamlined models that were also light. Raven, founded by Norman Wilkinson-Cox in the same decade, would prove another popular range of caravans. Wilkinson-Cox invented the screw-down corner steady, while Eccles would design the overrun brake system as used today. Bertram Hutchings Caravans was still making horse-drawn models, although by the mid-'20s demand had virtually disappeared. Hutchings also went into car-pulled caravans and constructed a few special motorhomes, while four-wheeled

Hutchings moved away from horse-drawn caravans to modern car designs, although this has a fashionable lantern roof and looks like a horse-drawn type.

living caravans – known as flats on wheels – were part of their portfolio as well. Hutchings would come into their own by the 1930s, branding their luxury caravans as Winchesters.

If you were a joiner or good at making things in general, you could design and build a non-prop (home-made caravan). Often these were crude, but some did look very professional. Some makers would begin like this right into the late 1950s in fact. The early DIY caravan builder sourced what they could to make a caravan for their own use. This practice became more popular in the 1930s and '50s, as mentioned. In fact, the Caravan Club had a competition at each national rally for such caravans. Elddis began in this way, with Siddle Cook designing a caravan and winning in 1963 at the national held at Longleat. The idea of home-builds stemmed mainly from the early 1920s, though odd attempts such as Frederick Alcock's caravan in 1912 were quite advanced in design.

So the caravanning craze was growing and the two new clubs, the Camping and Caravanning Club

Self-build caravan design and building began in the 1920s. Some were poor, while others, such as this, were made to a high standard.

and the Caravan and Motorhome Club, would also help in this growth. Owners would write to the manufacturers, such as Raven and Eccles, telling stories of how good their caravans had performed on tours of not just the UK but abroad as well. Some would take lengthy tours across Europe and further afield to India travelling roads that were barely usable. Manufacturers learnt a lot from these users, and Eccles, for instance, used their experiences to develop new ideas. Caravans for motorcyclists were designed, with Eccles and Raven being most prominent.

What was for sure was that the caravan had to be more affordable for the hobby to grow. This would be helped by the growth of car ownership in the next decade, the 1930s, during which middle-class folk would become car owners and also consider caravan holidays.

2.

Caravanning Comes to the Middle Classes

The 1930s was a massive turning point in caravanning; it was to be the decade that witnessed the first caravan rally, held at Minehead in 1932. Manufacturers used this rally as a springboard to show new designs and gauge reaction. But the rally also raised caravanning's profile and, again, the press was quick to get in on the act.

The 1930s was the beginning of art deco and the obsession with streamlining. New cars looked more attractive with this styling as the decade went on. The 1930s would also see a new breed of middle-class car owner, which in turn led to an increase in the number of new caravan owners.

The new decade would see the touring caravan become a permanent way of holidaying. From a rich man's pastime, the new breed of middle class with more disposable income and paid holidays would pave the way for a new industry. Although still small, it had much potential – so much so that the demand for caravans began to grow and

dedicated dealerships were founded. This in turn encouraged folk to go and look at the caravans and get advice from experienced salesmen. It also meant that dealers would set up hire fleets, allowing the caravan makers to concentrate on design and manufacturing and not on retail and hiring.

In 1932, *Caravan World* became the first magazine dedicated to the subject, with readers sending in articles on their trips at home and abroad. In May 1933, a new publication, *The Caravan & Trailer*, took over and would become the mouthpiece for the Caravan Club (now rebranded the Caravan and Motorhome Club)

Above: Car Cruisers lined up outside the factory ready to be dispatched to dealers. Manufacturers now mostly sold to dealers, who in turn also did hiring.

Opposite: The middle classes were becoming able to afford caravan holidays by the early 1930s, growing the leisure activity.

MAY, 1933
No. 1

Proprietor & Editor: F. L. M. HARRIS

SIXPENCE

The Only Magazine for those who love the Gipsy Life

The first edition of The Caravan & Trailer *magazine in May 1933. It cost 6d (2p in today's money!).*

as well as the few manufacturers. Adverts were eagerly added by caravan builders and also the new but small accessory market. One company that benefited from such growth was Eccles, which took full front-page ads with colourful alluring images that pulled in newcomers to the hobby. Print runs were initially around 3,000 but doubled to 6,000 as the 1930s progressed. Before this era *Autocar* published caravan news and articles as part of the motoring scene.

In 1927, Eccles moved from their old Gosta Green works to a new factory in Stirchley, near Birmingham. This was the first in the world dedicated to caravan and motorhome production and made the company market leaders, with makes such as Raven and Car Cruiser following. Motorhome production would later stop (see *The Motorhome Story*, The History Press). The company would produce luxury tourers and also more bread-and-butter models such as the 1935 Eccles Featherweight Four. Names such as Senator, National and Aristocrat would become good sellers.

The 1935 Eccles Featherweight four-berth with Riley tow car. Eccles were providing cheaper caravans as well as luxury models.

Dorothy Una Ratcliffe's Winchester on its 5,000-mile trip to South Africa. She wrote a book of her adventure in the early 1930s.

Winchester went 'streamlined' by 1930, as most caravans' insulation board was used with a canvas roof. They needed regular painting, but aluminium cost more.

Hutchings, which had now stopped horse-drawn production, went into streamlining and this proved a good move. Specials were also built under the company's Winchester brand, with many customers demanding bespoke layouts and specifications. One such customer, an author named Dorothy Una Ratcliffe, ordered her new Winchester directly from the works. Her idea was a 5,000-mile trip to South Africa, a real adventure back in the early 1930s. The trip proved

hazardous, with some of the worst floods seen in the area for fifty years washing away villages and bridges. The Winchester was christened 'Marigold', but Ratcliffe and her companion nearly lost their caravan in a flood as the banking where it was pitched collapsed within minutes of it being moved by local people. Ratcliffe wrote about it in her book, *South African Summer*. Overall, Ratcliffe was the author of forty-nine books, including many written about the Yorkshire Dales.

Caravanners going abroad in the 1930s were few, but those who did had to have their vehicle loaded via crane onto the ship.

Early caravanners went abroad if they could afford it, with the caravan being loaded onto a ship using a crane like the other cargo. Trips into Europe were taken and by the late 1930s some caravanners experienced a vastly changed Germany under the Nazi regime. The Europeans were also keen campers and their interest in caravanning was growing, with many of them buying UK-produced brands such as Eccles and Car Cruiser. Small concerns were beginning to produce caravans in Europe, with Dethleffs and Tabbert being early German makes, but the UK makers kept a firm grip on the growing market. Images of caravanners using the new German autobahns found their way into the motoring press, and this was good propaganda for the Nazi party.

With caravanning brought to the fore thanks to interest from the press and new manufacturers showing new designs, caravan sales saw further increases in the UK. In 1932, Eccles entered a caravan, towed by a Hillman Wizard, in the tough Monte Carlo Rally. This rigorous test saw the Eccles not only finish the course but also cross the line a very respectable 35th out of 110 competitors, boosting the company's reputation for design and quality. Eccles would also go on a testing endurance trip through the Sahara Desert, a feat for a solo car, never mind one towing a caravan. This was undertaken in 1935 using a Humber, with the Eccles Nymph equipped with metal shutters to deter theft and the crew armed with pistols for extra protection!

The Sunray "Gloucester."

3 Berth.   Suitable for 10 H.P. Car.

Above: The Eccles-Hillman car outfit with crew at the 1932 Monte Carlo Rally finished thirty-fifth: a good result.

Opposite: One of many new makers that appeared in the 1930s was Sunray. Many manufacturers folded in 1939, never to return.

Eccles' reputation was further enhanced by endurance runs such as this trans-Saharan trip in 1935. The tow car was a Humber.

The modern caravan now sported paraffin lights and cookers, along with 12V electric lighting running off the car battery. For entertainment a radio was fitted and even an under-floor bath. Car Cruiser caravans, under owner Major Flemming Williams, were still hiring caravans from their works at Thames Ditton. They were also capturing sales with their streamlined designs, which had been introduced in the 1920s but by the mid-'30s had become quite extreme, with curved rear sections and swept-back front ends giving the company's models a distinctive profile. Light weight and quality also sold the brand.

Williams' Car Cruisers led the way in streamlining. By the mid-1930s they had some quite extreme profiles.

10 ft. "Popular" Model.

Above: Raven were late to streamlined profiles, although by the mid-1930s this had changed. They were distinctive.

AN INTERIOR VIEW OF A FOUR BERTH CARAVAN WITH LANTERN ROOF AND WIRELESS SET

Above: A Car Cruiser interior from around 1937 classed as lightweight luxury. Note the built-in radio – very posh!

Right: Cheltenham (pictured), alias Summerfield, went more modern by the early 1930s, including the interiors.

Raven were quite slow to join the new streamlined era, using a rectangular profile with side-sloping roof that made their models look almost like railway goods trucks! However, by the mid-'30s new styling was introduced that saw curved front and rear ends being used, giving a more modern shape. Cheltenham caravans were also to enter into this new streamlined era with modern-looking tourers with interiors to match and mod cons such as a built-in radio.

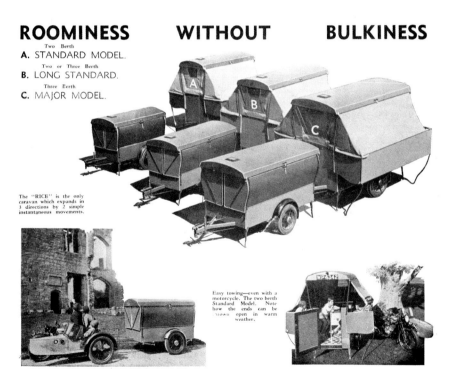

ROOMINESS WITHOUT BULKINESS

Two Berth
A. STANDARD MODEL.
Two or Three Berth
B. LONG STANDARD.
Three Berth
C. MAJOR MODEL.

The "RICE" is the only caravan which expands in 3 directions by 2 simple instantaneous movements.

Easy towing—even with a motorcycle. The two berth Standard Model. Note how the ends can be thrown open in warm weather.

Rice folding caravans were quite popular, being easy to store and tow in the 1930s.

Ace caravans launched in 1938 with lots of fuss. At £98 they were cheap and cheerful but the company faltered in late 1939. They even had their own caravan site in the woods next to the factory!

By the mid-'30s the number of small concerns building caravans was growing. In 1935, one maker in the Bournemouth area named Midland produced cheap caravans but sold them directly to the customer. The company were auctioneers but saw the rise in caravan demand and started to sell sub-standard caravans. However, this brand would become one of the biggest in Europe – Bluebird. The Knotts, who owned the company, would, by the mid-1940s, introduce a better-quality caravan, and they were producing more than 200 a week by the late '50s. Many manufacturers just produced a couple of caravans but then shut down, and this affected some potential buyers' confidence.

One name that was successful in producing extending caravans was Rice of Gargrave, Yorkshire. Their 1930s' design was really the folding camper of its day. The Rice was easy to tow even behind a motorbike and side car, such was its compact dimensions on the road. Rice made three models that found favour for several years.

Another 1930s maker, Ace Caravans, was all set to make an affordable yet good caravan for £98. The Ace was simple in design and was launched in grand style. The sales brochure was in the shape of the Ace caravan – a very innovative idea back then. However, the war began and Ace faded away never to return. Their simple interiors and single panelling was acceptable in the '30s at such a cheap price.

Four-wheel caravan designs had been around for many years but in trailer form, and a few manufacturers thought this was a good commercial idea. Thomson Caravans in Scotland in 1935 designed one to be pulled by a 10hp car! Eccles had also built several models to this idea, though mainly for showmen. Lancashire luxury builder Burlingham also built these four-wheel designs, but they did not catch on with the touring caravanner.

Eccles had used this idea in the late 1920s but this is a late '30s special. Showmen usually bought them.

Right: Thomson, the Falkirk caravan maker, built this 5.48m four-wheel model. This idea was also used by other manufacturers.

This big Thomson trailer, described below, can be towed by a 16-h.p. car

SCOTTISH-BUILT 4-WHEELER
A 3-Room 18-Footer

Below: One of the early established caravan dealerships, MG Caravans at Todmorden, began in the 1930s (picture taken in 1946).

Designed and manufactured by Clifford Dawtrey, the 1939 Coventry Steel Phantom Knight was a sensation with its steel panelling.

Dealerships began getting bigger, with names such as Yorkshire Caravans of Bawtrey, MG Caravans near Burnley and Round Stone caravans in Sussex all still around today. The new makers were keen to try out new ideas and designs, of which some were disasters while others were good ideas ahead of their time. Airlite was one such company, headed by Clifford Dawtrey. His ideas were excellent but the technology to carry them through successfully wasn't available and led to failure. He then set up Coventry Steel Caravans, designing and manufacturing the most aerodynamic caravan on the market in late 1938. In fact, it must have been a stunning innovation at the time as it is still striking today. However, the wooden frame

Rollalong were another early caravan maker who had some unique designs after the war.

with panel-beaten steel made it expensive and heavy, and the outbreak of war saw it scrapped. Only a few of this type were built, including a motorhome version.

New makers came and went in the 1930s, but others such as Siddall would be successful with their models, and makes such as Adams, Rollalong, Carlight, Cotswold, Car Trailers and Countryside would all make their mark. A car-body repair company called Bampton, based in Swindon, began building small extending caravans.

Above: This 1937 caravan fridge ran on gas. There was little room for food but it kept it relatively cool.

Left: Gas was a revolution for caravanners. From around 1936, Bottogas was being used but it meant the tank was on board in a seat locker.

The owners, brothers Reg and Ted Bampton, designed their little micro tourer, on which the sides extended out either end. It was a great design but with few dealers it never really got off the ground. Bampton built conventional caravans up to the early 1960s.

By the mid '30s, caravans generally had insulation, with luxury models having hot running water plus the new Bottogas, which was a tank usually in a locker that supplied gas to new gas lamps and a cooker. Heating by gas was also available. Soon a new supplier, Calor, was selling gas in bottles that caravanners could take to a stockist when empty and exchange for a full bottle for a fee. This saw paraffin lights and stoves dropped by manufacturers in favour of specially made gas ovens. By the late 1930s even a fridge had been designed especially for caravans that ran on gas.

The 1930s saw more caravan sites be established, such as this one in 1932 near Blackpool on the edge of the sand dunes.

The owners of this Eccles were, like many in this period, pitching on farmland with permission.

More caravan sites were established on coastlines near resorts. Some were lovely, while others were poorly run with mountains of rubbish and no proper sanitation. Soon new laws would need to be brought in and in 1939 a caravan body named the National Caravan Council was founded. The NCC would form a supply chain and also fight for caravan manufacturers and dealers. The Caravan Club of Great Britain also played its part and built up its membership in the 1930s.

Even though more sites became available, caravanners could still find farms on which to pitch. One caravanner told me many years ago that he would buy sweets for the farmer's children as a pitch fee. Sites would spring up especially on coasts and in places such as the Lake District and across Scotland. In the '30s the accessory market grew, with toilet tents (few folk used a loo in a caravan at this time) and Elsan toilets, plus even a caravan cot for babies as more families were taking up the hobby. All sorts of new gadgets were coming onto the market to

The accessory market was growing – this toilet tent was a popular purchase, even if a caravan had a utility room!

Caravanners— *Baby Problem* *Solved !*

FOLDED

With the **TRAVLKOT**

This Travlkot light cot was specially designed for caravanners with a young family and was easy to store!

fuel the growth of caravanning. Radios, baths and electric lighting were other improvements made during the decade.

In the meantime, the upper classes had not deserted caravanning; they embraced it within a niche luxury market sector. These were folk who would caravan all year round, with Christmas rallies organised by the Caravan Club.

> **Fun fact:** In the 1930s toilets were discouraged in caravans as they were seen as unhygienic and noisy!

The Dunlop Company developed new seating for caravans using Latex, claiming extra comfort over the old heavier sprung type. The fact that Dunlop was interested in this new leisure vehicle was a good sign that bigger industry was getting involved with the caravan supply chain. Chassis manufacturers began to spring up, so in many cases makers no longer made their own chassis.

For hardy caravanners, Christmas Club meets were an important part of the calendar.

Improvements in materials such as seating supplied by Dunlop made the caravanner more comfortable in their van.

However, there was a cloud on the horizon. The caravan movement had grown but now the Second World War was about to make big changes to the industry, as small as it was. Some manufacturers had seen the warnings and, like Eccles and Scottish maker Thomson, had designed special mobile offices for the Ministry of Defence.

When war was announced many caravan firms closed for good, while others decided to make what they could and go into war work. Thomson Caravans began making all types of war-related vehicles such as ambulances and trailers. Bill Riley's Eccles factory was also churning out war work in the shape of searchlight wagons and other vehicles. Coventry Steel developed an ambulance trailer that incorporated many of Dawtrey's ideas such as electric lighting and storage, making its ambulances more sophisticated and practical to use.

> **Fun fact:** It wasn't unheard of for a caravan to become detached from a vehicle due to the tow bar coming loose!

Caravans also became sought after as folk moved out from the cities to the countryside in fear of being bombed. Prices shot up and some caravans were terribly made using sacking for roofs and then painted. Many were sited in a farmer's field with several others, and some of these would never move and become used as static tourers after the war. Many caravan sites began in this way. Touring was not possible due to petrol shortages and nowhere being open. The war would help some manufacturers develop new methods of production, and Eccles would again benefit in this area.

The war saw caravans used as accommodation for workers at factories, and also on farms for land girls. They were placed on the outskirts of towns and cities safely out of the way. The NCC helped to allocate caravans on behalf of the government and many were lived in during this period. Caravans were in short supply and few were built due to lack of materials, but by the end of the war manufacturers were gearing up for production once again.

With the Second World War looming, caravan makers such as Eccles built these special units for use as mobile bases.

Right: Small caravan encampments evolved for war workers in the countryside. Note the tin helmets.

Below: In 1940, land girls take a break outside their Winchester. Caravans were in demand for accommodation for war workers.

Fun fact: Many caravanners used to throw the contents of their loo out into an open pit – summer was not good, smell-wise!

With the war coming to an end, the leisure caravan world began to reawaken and the 1940s saw some new manufacturers. The war had changed folk and the country had been economically devastated. Caravans from the '30s were often ornate and expensive, but to keep costs down an era of more functional caravans emerged. Eccles looked at faster, cheaper production ideas and quickly designed a post-war, 3.5m-long family caravan, naming it the Enterprise. It was a gamble for Eccles, who had built up a reputation for quality

A proud owner of one of the new Eccles Enterprises from 1947. Eccles made these in their hundreds using mass-production techniques learned from war work.

tourers by the end of the 1930s. However, built to a price and well put together using jig sections that kept costs down, the outcome was a caravan that took the market by storm. Eccles were quick to build up a new range based on this model.

Thomson also went mainly that way too, and new makers such as Berkeley and Paladin (Paladin had built a few examples pre-war) saw a new opening in cheaper but quality caravans. Many folk were war weary and basically needed a holiday. Many would hire a caravan and this led to a sales upsurge and new hire fleets being formed by dealers.

Other new makers such as Bailey and Alperson Products (later Sprite) began making caravans. However, Alperson's three Streamlites (Elf, Ranger and Rover) were still expensive at £600 each, and Sam and Harry Alper wanted a bigger slice of the boom market. In late 1949, Sam Alper visited dealers and found they wanted a cheap but good tourer that everybody who had a car could afford. He designed a caravan for less than £200, naming it the Sprite. He then proved its endurance capabilities

on several long-distance trips abroad; the new Newmarket factory was to make Sprites for export too as Sam sold some on his travels! By the end of the 1950s the Sprite became a range in its own right and was a top seller, with model names such as Aerial, Alpine and Musketeer. Sam Alper would go on to shape the caravan industry with innovative ideas and by marketing the caravanning lifestyle.

The next new name to emerge was Berkeley Caravans, owned by Charles Panter. He was a man of ideas, with fold-out caravans, extending models, some made out of steel and even a double-decker! His mind was always on the go and he would become a car manufacturer too.

Based at Biggleswade, Panter's factory would employ many from the area as his business took off. His first model, the Cara-partment, cost around £425 and had a front-end kitchen plus toilet room and rear dinette with a panel hinged to open up in sunny weather. Panter tried in vain to sell it in the US in the late 1940s, taking one out on tour, but nobody was interested and it also suffered limited sales in the UK.

Alperson Streamlite Rover, 1948. Sam Alper OBE was the co-founder of the firm with his brother Henry. It went on to make Sprites.

Charles Panter's first caravan after the war. Former furniture maker Panter launched his Cara-partment and went on to make Berkeley sports cars.

Postcards from sites visited on holiday were sent to friends. Some were quite elaborate, including this one with a tiny concealed notebook.

A photo of a stopover in 1947 from a caravanner's album. The café and site has gone but the premises are still used as a garage.

Another social history snippet from the same album with the Cheltenham caravan the photographer probably used parked on the drive of the folk they visited.

With the war over, there would be a new uptake in caravanning, and many caravanners would begin logging their travels with photos taken on the trip. These would be put together in an album to look back over on winter evenings. Caravanners would visit friends and relatives and take photos of people as well as their pets. If a good site was found, a photo was taken to remind them and show to others. Postcards of sites stopped on were often sent to friends – some were quite amateur, while others had a little notebook in the card.

The next decade would see caravanning take off with more sites, better-equipped caravans and cheaper models. Also, the 1950s would be the start of 'off the peg' tow bars, making the towing of caravans safer and easier.

3.

Caravanning and the Working-Class Holiday

The new decade of the 1950s was to witness a boom in caravanning; folk wanted to get away and caravans were seen as ideal. New ideas in manufacturing would be tried including glass-fibre mouldings, which allowed more pleasing shapes and added durability. The new breed of cars also boasted more power, plus there was a new manufacturer of purpose-designed tow bars and electrics. Colin Witter set up a Chester engineering company that looked at the growing market of caravan and trailer ownership. Working with some car manufacturers, he set about designing bars that met approval and could be produced on a commercial, off-the-shelf basis.

Dixon and Bate, another Chester-based company, had been making trailers for cars since 1921, but they too would take to making and designing tow bars. It would be Witter, though, that took the market. The company increased production throughout the 1950s and also improved the electrical systems. Witter no doubt helped the caravan market, making the tow bar

safer than the days of blacksmiths, garages and engineering works. Mass-produced bars with cheaper price tags were what was needed, and Colin Witter made that happen.

The new breed of caravanner wanted a cheaper tourer, one they could afford and tow easily. As well as the Alperson Sprite detailed in the previous chapter, other makers that did well were Berkeley, Marston, Lynton, Paladin and Willerby, all mass-market brands with new ideas. Eccles added new models, keeping a tight hold on their market share, although the new makers were making an impact. Bill Knotts's Bluebird Caravans had grown into a large concern with a growing portfolio, including park homes, motorhomes and holiday caravans. Knott could buy in bulk, keeping prices keen.

Above: Colin Witter was an engineer who in the early 1950s revolutionised tow-bar design and manufacture. (Courtesy Witter)

Opposite: By the early 1950s Witter Towing Brackets was established. Here bars are ready for dispatch. (Courtesy Witter)

In 1950 Sam Alper began his Sprite brand of value-for-money caravans that cost £199 and brought caravanning to the working class.

A Willerby Heatherbelle tourer in the late 1950s. Willerby established the Hull area for caravan manufacturing in 1946.

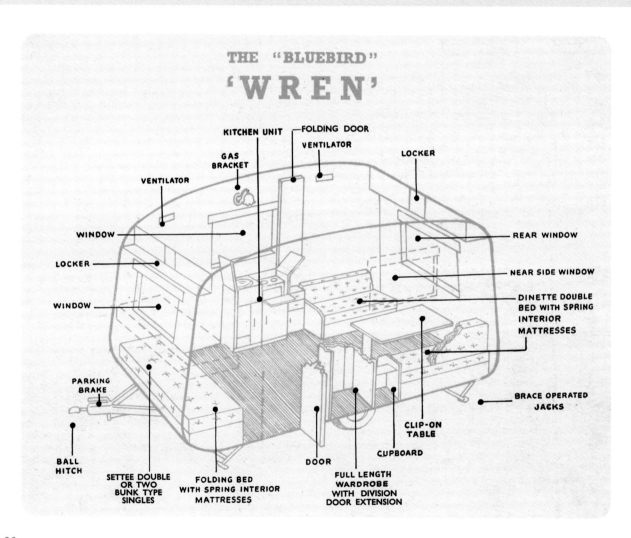

THE "BLUEBIRD"
'WREN'

KITCHEN UNIT

FOLDING DOOR

VENTILATOR

GAS BRACKET

LOCKER

VENTILATOR

WINDOW

REAR WINDOW

LOCKER

NEAR SIDE WINDOW

WINDOW

DINETTE DOUBLE BED WITH SPRING INTERIOR MATTRESSES

PARKING BRAKE

BRACE OPERATED JACKS

CLIP-ON TABLE

BALL HITCH

CUPBOARD

SETTEE DOUBLE OR TWO BUNK TYPE SINGLES

FOLDING BED WITH SPRING INTERIOR MATTRESSES

DOOR

FULL LENGTH WARDROBE WITH DIVISION DOOR EXTENSION

Above: Cheltenham Caravans used glass fibre to their advantage, with the Stag from 1957 featuring a glass-fibre roof.

Opposite: The Bluebird Wren was one of many models made by Bluebird Caravans. Owner Bill Knott became a millionaire by the end of the 1950s.

Right: Charles Panter's glass-fibre-bodied Berkeley Delight from 1956–57 showing its prototype development. It had limited success.

Below: The Vogue from Willerby that was launched for 1957 was heavy and expensive; around 115 were made.

VOGUE 14' 4 BERTH

This new caravan, constructed in Willerby Armourplast, is an important development in glass-fibre reinforced plastics. No joints . . . so it never leaks! Shell and chassis in one moulded construction for utmost rigidity. This new material has a high finish and is virtually indestructible. Ideal as a fast tourer in all weather conditions, its special feature which will delight the touring enthusiast is the large 'see through' windows (see illustration on cover). The insulation is excellent owing to the special qualities of the material used. An air space is left between the inner and outer shells. This caravan is available with 3 alternative layouts!

This view shows clearly the clean lines, the large 'see through' windows, the easy clean surfaces, the ample storage space and neat built-in roof lockers.

One market sector was changing, however: the hand-built luxury tourer was still in demand, but higher prices saw fewer new buyers. Winchester would become more expensive and yet the design had changed little. Cheltenham Caravans saw the challenge of cheaper caravans and, in an effort to keep their tourers special, the Gardener family looked at glass fibre, also called GRP. This new material was expensive but durable and relatively easy to repair if damaged. In 1956, Cheltenham used a GRP mould for its caravan roofs, followed a year or so later by front- and end-moulded panels, giving its caravans a distinctive profile.

Willerby, the Hull maker, launched its Vista and Vogue in GRP but to lesser success. Berkeley also launched its version, the Delight, but owner Charles Panter's production methods used two moulded halves, then joined them in the middle. Paladin also dabbled with the idea, while Freeman went over to GRP along with Siddall, both luxury makers. Cheltenham, Carlight and Siddall probably best used GRP to its potential.

The 1950s sites were getting a little more planned, with marked pitches and spaces – plus the grass was cut more often!

Caravanners were venturing further afield using the new ferries from Dover to Calais by the mid-1950s.

Cost, though, was a problem – luxury makers could get away with charging extra, whereas those trying to produce cheaper models with GRP could not.

The 1950s caravanner was far better catered for, with better caravans, more choice and also cheaper models. Sites were also slowly getting their act together with new sites being planned with better facilities, although many were still caravans pitched in a field. Sites abroad were more often being developed to the standard of UK ones, and both this and the now drive-on ferry meant caravanners could get to the Continent for a holiday.

The caravan movement was to gain more publicity on account of Sam Alper's endurance runs, during which he sold his caravans and built up an export market. Alper thought it was a good idea for all manufacturers to prove how well their caravans were made and that the public should be able to witness this. Eccles, who were no strangers to testing their caravans pre-war, built a special Coronet-based tourer that was taken to South America on an expedition. It had to cross rivers, so it had to be amphibious too! However, the idea of caravan testing in a competition appealed.

In 1954, a caravan endurance event was held with the help of the Caravan Club. The idea was to encourage car manufacturers to get in on this new event. Towing competitions were set up, along with braking, reversing, hill climbs and obstacle courses.

Eccles were still the leaders in the 1950s. This special Coronet was made for an expedition to South America.

The Eccles was also tested for floating as part of the special specification.

Left: A Cheltenham and Jaguar on the night run of the first British Caravan Road Rally in 1954.

Below: Ingrid Bergman borrows a Paladin tourer from dealers Harringtons in 1958 for location filming in North Wales.

NO BETTER WAY, SAYS INGRID

FILM actress Ingrid Bergman meets caravan specialist Arthur Heap and Mrs. Heap of W. D. Harrington & Co., Delamere. Harringtons provided four caravans for the use of the stars of the film "Inn of the Sixth Happiness" when it was recently filmed in North Wales. And Miss Bergman says: "I can think of no better way of seeing the beauty of North Wales than by having a caravan."

Dealers and caravan manufacturers joined the event, with many such as Cecil Gardener of Cheltenham and Charles Panter of Berkeley getting involved by driving themselves.

The public could watch for free and the British Caravan Road Rally was a success; it was agreed that it should be a yearly event. Health and safety didn't come into it at all, yet until its demise in the mid-1970s nobody was seriously injured or killed. Throughout its existence manufacturers learnt lessons on towing stability, build and aerodynamics.

The Witter Towing Bracket Company got great coverage from these events and the touring caravan was brought more to the public's attention. Several chassis manufacturers now supplied the growing tourer market, these being B&B Trailers (which later became Ak-Ko) and Peak Trailers. These two basically supplied the trade, although other makers such as Bowden Trailers also had a smaller share along with Angus Engineering.

Many of the old dealers such as Harringtons in Cheshire were growing in size, hiring, selling, repairing caravans and also supplying the odd film star with a caravan on location, such as Ingrid Bergman in 1958.

Caravan rallies were popular with Caravan Club members. These were events held mainly on weekends with local club members from a county getting together. Many friendships were made and these events were very social, with games for the children and adults too. Bonfire night and Christmas rallies were organised as well. The facilities were typically basic – there was no loo but there was a standpipe for water with a waste pit usually dug by the organisers.

The manufacturers also had loyal customers, with Cheltenham forming their own owners' club in 1950. They became and still are one of the oldest clubs of a one-make caravan that is still going in modern times. Other manufacturers' owners' clubs would follow, especially in the 1960s.

Caravanning in the '50s also saw micro models become a popular choice, such as Berkeley's Caravette costing £100 in 1954 and the Paladin Pixie of 1953, Sprite Colt and Penguin. The 1950s was a time when you could still park your car and tourer in a side street of a town and go and do some shopping – traffic was light back then! With petrol rationing lifted in the early '50s folk were touring more. Most would stop over at a place for a day or two and then move on.

Caravan Club centre rallies were to become very popular, with children and adults joining in. This is a club rally in around 1965.

The 1954 Berkeley Caravette was another Panter design for micro caravanning; it could be converted to a normal trailer, too.

Opposite: The Paladin Pixy from 1952 was a micro family tourer. Paladin also built holiday and mobile homes.

Memories

My grandparents Charlie and Annie Jenkinson (Nana, sat in the centre, with grandad stood behind), who caravanned from the 1950s, made many friends on their trips. This photo was taken around 1960 at a meet-up of caravanning friends.

(Charlie and Annie Jenkinson)

The 1950s, though, would see the demise of some older names. Burlingham at Garstang had produced luxury tourers, some novel such as the Sportsman complete with a boat on the roof. Winchester were purchased by Stirling luxury caravan makers and closed down, while Siddall were taken over by the Gailey Group. Eccles would be bought out by Sam Alper in 1960. The world was changing – the 1960s saw a new breed of car with caravans to match. Fold-up caravans were still relatively popular, but with the new Austin Mini more folders would be brought to market.

Sprite, with Eccles, was now a formidable force. The Eccles factory was shut and a new plant was built at Newmarket, Suffolk, with Sprite. The Eccles brand had lost its way by 1960, so Alper brought in young designer Reg Dean to relaunch it to modern standards. Dean did this for 1962 with stunning results, using the latest ideas in domestic interior design and contemporary and distinctive new thinking for the exteriors. Eccles were back on the map and by 1963 Sprite Eccles merged with Bluebird after months of

The 1954 Burlingham Sportsman De-Luxe two-berth – oh and that is a boat on the roof!

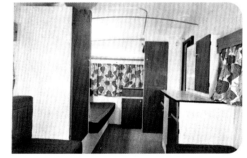

Moonstone "B" Mk. 2 interior

The new-look Eccles was the work of top caravan designer Reg Dean, who wasn't afraid to use contemporary ideas in touring caravans.

The old Eccles factory paint shop at Stirchley in its heyday in 1955. By 1961, production was moved to Sprite's Newmarket base in Suffolk to a recently acquired factory named The Pines, originally set up to produce Sprite boats.

speculation, forming Caravans International (Ci), the UK's biggest maker, and by the mid-1960s, also Europe's.

The accessory market was an area that Ci also went big on, spreading its wings in a very fast-expanding market sector. By this period the Caravan Show was established at Earls Court after being part of the Motor Show. This was the shop window for the caravan industry for retail and trade. Held in November, it was the show where manufacturers made sure they got a stand. This period saw the Ci group expand into Europe, with factories producing for a hungry market. The Ci stand was always packed with new models and cut-out sections of caravans showing how they were made.

Earls Court Caravan Show in 1968. Ci had a big stand with all their brands on display, including this open-sided Eccles Topaz.

Memories

Roger Williams: One of several caravans my parents owned included this new 1964 Sprite Musketeer. Taken in the summer of that year, this was on one of our frequent trips to the New Forest. There were five of us, which meant we could all fit in Dad's 1961 Austin Westminster A99. In 1965 we went to the Costa Brava for two weeks!

Rogers Williams' family with their new 1964 Sprite Musketeer.

The Sprite Alpine had by the early 1960s become one of the most popular caravans on the road. Its 3.68m length could squeeze in up to five, while its weight unladen was 558kg, meaning the average family saloon car could pull it. Its bigger brother, the 4.42m Musketeer, gave extra space and was popular with larger families, being the second-best seller. Thomson, the Scottish maker, was the second largest in the UK, producing its Glen series of quality-built, medium-priced tourers in a large factory in Falkirk. Thomson also had an owners' club, which it founded in 1964. The Scottish tourers were well liked south of the border and the brand exported their quality tourer range all over Europe. Willerby Caravans had been founded in 1946 in Willerby near Hull, and by the late

Right top: By 1964 the Sprite Alpine was the top seller in UK. It provided great value as it was basic but ideal for new caravanners.

Right bottom: Many caravan manufacturers had owners' clubs by the early 1960s, including big Scottish maker Thomson. The first owners' rally was held in 1964.

go ahead) go sprite '68

sprite value sets you free!

The 1968 Ci Sprite Musketeer was another of Sprite's top sellers. It offered extra space for families yet was lightweight and distinctive with its swan-neck roofline.

1950s several other manufacturers had set up in the area – mainly ex-Willerby employees. These new concerns were Cresta, Astral, Lissett, Robin and Welton.

By 1965, new makers Ace, Mardon, Silverline, Alpine Coach, Belmont and Swift had joined the new nucleus of Hull caravan manufacturers. By the end of the decade, Hull and the surrounding area was the biggest centre of caravan production in the UK, making tourers and holiday caravans. The 1960s spawned a big explosion in tourer demand, not just in the UK but in Europe as well, with manufacturers exporting caravans into Europe using Hull docks. Across the Humber in

Founded in late 1964, Swift was a small maker and one of many in Hull. Ken Smith, the founder, worked hard to establish his range.

Cosalt in Grimsby founded Humber Abbey Caravans. The Humber name was later dropped and Abbeys became much sought-after tourers. This is a shot of the factory in the late 1960s on final cleaning and inspection of the tourers before dispatch.

Les Marshall had worked for Willerby but by 1962 had set up Mardon. They initially made micro caravans but eventually built larger models.

150 Astral caravans in the mid-1960s lined up at Hull docks waiting to be exported to Europe.

Grimsby, the Cosalt Group, which made cold-insulated containers, began producing caravans in 1966. Using a large marquee as a temporary factory to begin with, the renamed Humber Caravan Co. produced its Abbey range of medium-priced tourers and holiday homes. The Humber name was changed to Abbey Caravans after the Humber Car Co. objected.

The accessory market had extended in the early 1960s, with such products as portable TVs with rechargeable batteries. New sleeping bags were now cheaper and lighter, while new 12V strip lighting was also introduced. This side of the market would grow dramatically over the decade and there were soon all sorts of caravanning bits available, including winches for getting your caravan up your drive such as the Sammy Winch. This was made in Wales, with many other items also made in the UK. There were awnings and water containers, the most well known of the latter being the Aquaroll. In addition, there were hobs with grills and ovens, and gas-flame fires.

CARAVAN T.V.!

The new transistorised TV that is truly portable, and can be operated by rechargeable internal battery, car battery, or A.C. mains. Ideal as your portable second set in the home, to take on your holiday, for boat-lovers, those living in caravans, etc. Versatile 12-channel tuning. 8¾" screen. Twenty-five transistors, 13 diodes. Wt. 22 lb, including battery. Telescopic aerial. Measurements—10½" x 10½" x 13". Earphone sockets fitted for private use with special earphone attachment with 10 ft lead.

Rechargeable batteries:
2 x Exide 3MFB7. Price £5 4s 0d per pair.

OPERATES FROM BATTERIES

★

A BOON TO MAINS-LESS CARAVANNERS

★

59 gns.
inc. tax.
(batteries extra)

Send for further details to:

LITTLEWOOD'S RADIO LTD

161 LANGWORTHY ROAD
SALFORD 6 · LANCS.

TEL. PENdleton 4340

Far left: In the early 1960s this portable TV was what you had to entertain you on your caravanning trips.

Left: Sleeping bags were a must for caravanners; there were a lot of makers and different grades for warmth.

Above: If you had a steep drive or were in a tight spot, the Sammy Winch was possibly the answer!

Right: Fylde Caravans were typical of small but thriving dealerships. There were many around the UK like this.

With this period seeing many new dealerships establish from small concerns to larger ones, it was common to have several dealers within a few miles of each other. Some dealerships grew, such as the Gailey Group, who mostly had indoor showrooms with suited salesmen, making caravan buying a more professional affair and more like buying a new car. With new producers, new dealers were needed, while established companies such as Ci had around 150 in the UK.

Awnings and Aquaroll water containers were popular in this period.

A Gailey showroom in 1968 with a salesman ready to confirm a deal with the couple. This was the scene in larger dealerships, which had the feel of a car showroom.

With new manufacturers, some dealerships would have up to twelve brands stocked. South African 'Gypsy' caravans were renamed as Viking Fibreline for the UK market and began production in 1964 near Carlisle. Built using GRP moulds, they were well built and distinctive, and sold well. Sylva Caravans, an Irish maker, was another foreign maker that tried its luck in the UK. It began around 1964 but had finished building caravans by 1971.

The Sylva tourer was built in Ireland and exported to the UK from 1965.

Memories

Peter Washington: This is one of several caravans my dad had; it was a 1966 Astral Ranger, which we picked up from the factory in Hull! It was well travelled, and we went all over the Continent with it. Our tow car here was a 1967 Hillman Hunter but we towed it with several different cars.

Peter Washington's parents' 1966 Astral Ranger.

A lone 1965 Sprite Alpine on a small site at Moy, near Banavie, with Ben Nevis in the background. This idyllic pitch was typical of the period. Scotland was a major caravanning destination for many. (Courtesy of Andrew Craven)

In the 1960s you could still pull up outside a pub with your tourer and have a pint – something not endorsed in the modern day! (1967 Cavalier tourer and Mk2 Cortina GT.)

New car models launched in the 1960s meant there were plenty of decent tow cars, including the Rover 2000, Triumph 2000, Ford Cortina and Volvo Amazon (the newer Volvos became a firm tow-car favourite in the 1970s). The humble caravan site saw more transformation and added shops, amusements, swimming baths, bin areas and proper toilets and shower blocks. The British Caravan Road Rally was in full swing in the '60s; now a big event in the industry's calendar with caravan racing and tough rally routes that saw many caravans smashed to pieces in the process.

For those touring with their caravans in the 1960s, Scotland would be seen as a favourite destination, with caravanners stopping overnight by lochs, while the Lake District and the Yorkshire Dales were other top destinations.

By the end of this decade, the era of stopping over in a lay-by for a pint or two was virtually over due to new laws.

Fun fact: Caravanners sometimes stopped in a lay-by for lunch and it wasn't unheard of for other folk to ask if they were a snack bar!

Several car models would become favourites among caravanners, such as the Wolseley (pictured above with a 1963 Astral tourer).

Some caravan sites had very efficient receptions in the late 1960s!

An Eccles/Mercedes outfit competing on the track section of the British Caravan Road Rally event. Note the hasty front repair job – many caravans would be written off.

4.

Boom and Bust – The Touring Caravan Faces New Challenges

The caravan boom of the 1960s was to continue into the new decade, although there were to be many changes to the way folk used their leisure time that would impact on the touring caravan market.

By 1970 the UK caravan industry was virtually at its peak. Many new makers were to launch, mainly from the Hull area, such as Beverley Coach Craft, Tranby, Eaton, Castle, Haltemprice, Royden, Buccaneer, Elite, Windsor, Riviera, Minster, Churchill and many others. Names from the 1960s such as Elddis and Mardon, along with Swift, Silverline and Ace, would expand into new factories as the boom continued. But Car Cruiser, which had been there at the start, had passed through several owners and was eventually

A 1971 Beverley Coach Craft 455, from one of the many Hull makers to hit the caravan scene in the early 1970s. Paddy McMahon, the champion show jumper, was loaned this Beverley for shows.

Car Cruiser Cameo 2 from 1971. The brand had sadly faded away by this period after being one of the leaders and pioneers.

Earls Court, the biggest show of the year, in November 1970. This is the Lynton stand prior to opening day, showing new 1971 tourer and holiday home models.

bought by Bob Cooper at Cooper Coachworks. A few failed attempts to bring the brand back meant that by 1972 the name had gone forever. At this time there were to be more caravan shows, the NEC being one from the 1980s, while Glasgow also had a big one at the SECC. However, Earls Court would remain the main event until the late 1980s.

Ci Group were now Europe's, if not the world's, biggest manufacturer of leisure vehicles, but the boom also saw stronger competition from abroad with Adria, Tabbert, Kabe, Knaus, Hobby and Cabby all trying to dig into the UK market of 60,000 tourers sold in 1972. Ci made half this number, while other UK makers such as A Line, Astral and Ace contributed to the total.

Kabe of Sweden was one of several imported makes to try to crack the UK market in the early 1970s. Cost and UK tastes saw them fail.

Caravanners were always keen to possess the newest accessories and the 1970s saw cassette radios and TVs being fitted. Japanese brands such as Hitachi, Toshiba, JVC, Sony, Teleton and Sharp were making 12V portable TVs that were lighter with larger screens than the models from the previous decade. Portable aerials also hit the market, although TV coverage was still hit and miss in many areas. Caravans were becoming more like homes on wheels!

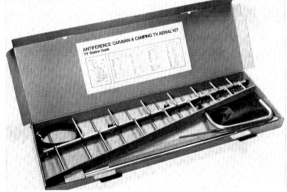

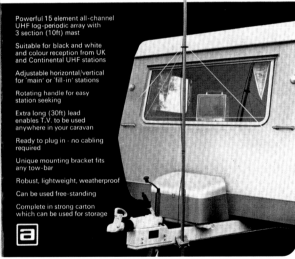
TVs in tourers became a must-have for many owners. TV aerial kits were marketed so caravanners didn't miss their telly!

Once you had found a picture you could sit back and watch your new black-and-white portable – until the car battery went!

Right: Towing mirrors were available in all sorts of designs. The Retrovisor was a periscope so the driver could see through the caravan window behind!

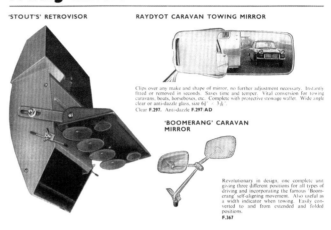

Towing mirrors

'STOUT'S' RETROVISOR

RAYDYOT CARAVAN TOWING MIRROR

Clips over any make and shape of mirror, no further adjustment necessary. Instantly fitted or removed in seconds. Saves time and temper. Vital conversion for towing caravans, boats, horseboxes, etc. Complete with protective stowage wallet. Wide angle clear or anti-dazzle glass, size 6¼" / 3⅞".
Clear **F.297**. Anti-dazzle **F.297/AD**

'BOOMERANG' CARAVAN MIRROR

Revolutionary in design, one complete unit giving three different positions for all types of driving and incorporating the famous 'Boomerang' self-aligning movement. Also useful as a width indicator when towing. Easily converted to and from extended and folded positions.
F.367

Below: Roof-mounted wind deflectors were quite popular until the early 1980s, but did they help save fuel?

Warm woollen hats come in many colours.

■ Lady's anorak of a quilted nylon material. This garment looks smart and is practical.

CLOTHES FOR CARAVANNING CHECKLIST

Before you go wild at your local clothing store, work out what sort of caravanning is your speciality. Are you a summer's day only man —or do you love tramping around farm sites? This will obviously affect your choice of say, gumboots or sandals. Now read on to see our selection:—

Leather Fell Boots	£3	5s	0d
Suede Fell Boots	£2	9s	11d
TUF Bush Boots	£2	19s	11d
Waterproof Nykon Boots	£3	19s	11d
PVC Gum Boots	£1	19s	11d
Dunlop Boots	£2	3s.	6d
Anorak	£4	19s	11d
Lady's Anorak	£4	19s	0d
Track Suits from	£3	5s	0d
Levis Jeans (Male)	£3	10s	0d
Flared cord Jeans	£4	9s	11d
Lee Riders Jeans (Female)	£4	15s	0d
Cotton Jeans	£3	19s	6d
Non-crease Jeans	£4	19s	11d
Terron cotton shirt	£2	2s	6d
Denham Monument shirt	£2	2s	6d
Tee shirt (sh/sleeves)		8s	11d
Tee shirt (lng/sleeves)	£1	5s	0d
Cotton polo necked shirt		12s	11d
Woollen pom pom hat		12s	11d
Cotton Long Johns		19s	11d

Slammer', although it's doubtful whether they had much effect! There was also the electric water pump that ran off 12V and would be fitted to most tourers by the mid-'70s. The awning market had grown as new makes and easier and lighter designs hit the market.

Left: If you wanted to be a trendy caravanner in the 1970s you had to have an anorak and woollen bobble hat, really!

Below: This hair dryer from the early 1980s used gas and probably wouldn't pass safety checks today!

There were masses of accessories available, such as extending towing mirrors and a periscope you put on the car roof so the driver could see through the caravan windows at the front *and* rear for traffic behind. To help the aerodynamics, rooftop wind deflectors could be fitted and one make that was quite popular was 'the Wind

MORCO Mistral...
the Caravanner's Hairdryer

complete with
RONSON Escort 2000
accessories.
R.R.P. £20.70
plus V.A.T.

Bernie the Bolt! The Golden Shot *TV game show in the 1970s offered big prizes. Host Bob Monkhouse watches a 1970 Lynton Arrow being brought into the studio. (Courtesy of the Dean family)*

Clothing designed for caravanners hit the market, including lightweight waterproofs and smart jackets. A hair dryer by gas caravan appliance maker Morco was classed as the

Hand-built luxury tourers such as the 1977 Stirling became less popular as they looked dated and expensive.

caravanner's friend. Caravanning's popularity saw even TV game shows such as *The Golden Shot* hosted by Bob Monkhouse feature a tourer as first prize. Lynton Caravans were one of several manufacturers to offer one of their models as a prize, giving the firm good publicity.

Fun fact: In some tourers, condensation was so bad in colder weather that towels had to be placed under the windows.

The hand-built luxury caravan market was well catered for with the likes of Safari, Welton, Castleton, Carlight, Royale, Ensor, Cheltenham, Stirling and Viking. This market was slowly beginning to shrink; although hand-built and having an air of status on site and road, the designs were looking old fashioned. However, there were still older caravanners around who wanted to own one of these brands.

Plus, in the 1960s and early '70s there were several DIY caravan shells. These were glass-fibre shells mounted on a chassis, then left bare for the buyer to fit out themselves. Several makers were around such as Wake and Sapphire but more common was Vanmaster. This was to be the most successful and today these still turn up discarded in gardens and farmers' fields.

A 40mph speed limit for caravans had been in force since the 1960s, but the talk from 1970 was of increasing this to 50mph. It was decided that from July 1972 all trailers including caravans would have to have warning reflective triangles fitted on the rear panel. From 1971 all caravan manufacturers fitted them in readiness for the new legislation, while some companies such as Fisher fitted them from a year earlier. The speed limit was raised in 1973, but the tow car had to have a sticker in its front window showing the car's kerb weight. The caravan also had to display a sticker in the window showing its weight, but nobody checked these additions. Many, like my dad, did put the 50mph sticker (a requirement) on the back of the caravan, taking off the 'Sorry, I'm stuck to 40' speed limit sticker!

Vanmaster offered DIY shells for caravanners to add furniture to, but this practice fell by the wayside by the late 1970s.

An ad by one-time car electrics giant Lucas regarding retrofitting warning triangles – the law by July 1972.

Memories

Martin Cooling: My dad had several caravans over the years, but the one we liked the most was a 1975 A Line Super 1300. My uncle also had an A Line. We loved that tourer and it took us on many great holidays. But after a year we had to sell it as it proved too heavy for my dad's Ford Cortina 1300 Mk2 estate.

Martin Cooling's parents' A Line 1300.

By the late 1970s the DIY shell had gone out of fashion, and home-built caravans too. The market was big in tourers but, due to the level of competition, manufacturers came and went. The big Hull tourer makers were Astral, Willerby (making Robin tourers), A Line and Ace. In the north-west of England, there was a thriving but smaller industry of caravan manufacture. Lunar, Knowsley, Ski, Fleetwind and Trophy were based around Preston and Wigan.

In September of each year manufacturers would show their wares. This meant that around Hull factories were open for trade, or some used a local pub or hotel. By 1975 it was decided that the Lawns in Cottingham on the edge of Hull should be a venue for makers to group together so trade didn't have to travel from factory to factory. By 1983 a public open weekend was launched that became a popular event.

In 1972, a decade after owner Terry Reed had founded the company, Ace Caravans joined up with neighbouring static manufacturers Belmont Caravans, forming Ace Belmont International (ABI). This made the Beverley firm second only to Ci. Within two years ABI would add Elddis in County Durham to their portfolio and launch a new entry-level range for 1973 called Monza and aimed directly at Sprite. Competing Sprites were £25 cheaper but the Monza finish and build were excellent. In 1973, Ci decided to head for solus dealerships, followed by ABI years later.

The interior of a 1971 Lunar Saturn, one of several north-west manufacturers in this period.

Introducing the surprising new Monza touring range.

If you thought that all touring caravans were either too expensive or cheaply made, you're in for a surprise with new Monza Tourers.

First surprise is the superb, distinctive exterior styling executed in pressed aluminium panels for touring lightness and strength.

Next surprises are the veneer edged furniture, carpet throughout, full kitchen units (including stainless sink and drainer) and many more.

The surprising new Monza range features 6 models from 10ft. to 14ft.

And here's the biggest surprise of all: Monza Tourers start at £389 !

Get full details of the surprising new Monza range soon.

MONZA
a whole new standard in touring caravans

Monza Caravans,
Swinemoor Lane, Beverley, East Yorkshire

A Member of the Ace Belmont International Group.   MC11/72

The entry-level ABI Monza range for 1973 was a big hit with buyers, eventually stealing Sprite sales by the late 1970s.

B&B SOLVES THE PROBLEM

Now you don't have to get up to back up

with the new B&B Sigma 'Back-Up' System

B & B Trailers, leaders for more than a quarter of a century in caravan towing equipment, are first in the field with the introduction of the revolutionary Sigma reversing system.

No longer do you have to leave the driver's seat or flick switches to back-up your van, because the Sigma system takes care of everything automatically.

So, before you choose your next van make sure it is B & B equipped and stay up to date.

All of a sudden you could reverse your tourer with the new Sigma reverse system, but you had to learn how to first!

The caravan buyer now had more choice than ever, and with a new auto reverse system developed by B&B trailers for 1974, caravanners now could reverse their vehicles easier without having to get out and disengage the overrun brake system.

Fun fact: Putting up a caravan awning was often a major area for dispute between husband and wife!

Another idea was devised in the 1950s by caravanners wanting to protect their caravan's front from stone chips when under tow. This was to tie a large canvas sheet to the front panel. By the 1970s, front-protection covers could be purchased to protect the aluminium panels, but as GRP was used more on tourers the need evaporated. The last few years has seen a resurgence of this practice with designer covers, mainly developed for Bailey when their early Alu-Tech models were prone to dents on the front panel. Since then, covers have been seen on all makes of caravan.

In April 1973 VAT had been brought in and this saw caravan prices rise. In addition, the oil crisis and rising inflation saw caravan prices go up even further.

The upshot was that in the mid-'70s sales began to fall and by 1974–75 sales were down to 40,000. Several makers folded, including Cheltenham and Ensor, followed by Welton. The Sprite market, though, was quite buoyant and this saw makers such as clubman makers Avondale, Astral, Silverline, Bailey and Abbey produce new, cheaper ranges to keep sales moving. Although caravanners were able to go abroad more easily, the cheap package holiday lured folk to the sun and sales declined even more. Sprite stood its ground and Ci ploughed money into TV advertising to boost sales.

Memories

Andrew Jenkinson: Yes, this is my dad outside our Elddis Tornado on a lovely site at Leintwardine in June 1970. That's me coming out age 12 – I loved that week. The site was in an orchard, just me and my sister, Mum and Dad. I feel emotional just thinking about the lovely time we had. The site is still there.

Andrew Jenkinson's parents' Elddis in 1970.

Above: The Witter Towbars entry in the road rally of 1975, with the inflation-beating Ci Sprint 12 priced at less than £1,000. (Courtesy of Witter Towbars)

Right: The 1973 limited edition Sprite Alpine C, made to celebrate twenty-five years of Sprite caravans.

Left: Ci had their own finance company in the 1970s, offering caravanners credit for buying a caravan and accessories etc.

In 1973, Ci's Sprite brand celebrated twenty-five years, and to mark the occasion the company produced a special 'Silver Jubilee' version of their best-selling Alpine C model, priced at £615. They made around 135, and the models included carpet, water pump, 12V lighting and silver exterior graphics. The firm

Reg Dean promoting his 1981 A Line Imps with two young women at the factory. Dean was a top caravan designer.

would also introduce their own finance company for caravanners wanting to buy a new Ci tourer, awning or Ci-related accessories. A used Ci warranty was also introduced – a first for the industry.

Ci also launched its Ci Sprint for 1975. Costing less than £1,000, it was a five-berth, 3.4m long and weighed 457kg, making it towable by a Mini. The build involved cost cutting and it was followed by a larger model in 1976. Ci would launch its Cadet Ten in September 1978 for 1979, which was designed to be towed by Ford's then new Fiesta. A Line in Hull responded with a clone of the Cadet named the Imp, designed by Reg Dean, but it didn't have the same success. Dean had a string of successes in caravan design behind him, working for Sprite, Lynton, ABI, A Line, Deanline and eventually back to ABI in 1985. He was a brilliant caravan/holiday caravan designer with strong attention to detail. The front cover of this book is a Lynton from 1972, one of his designs, and the woman who featured in the company brochures became his wife!

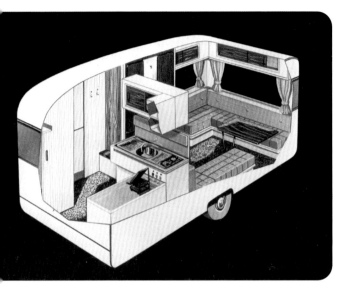

Above: A Ford Cortina Lotus Mk1 as it competes in the British Caravan Road Rally brake test with a 1970 Lynton Tomahawk. This event was at the height of its popularity in this period.

Left: Cavalier's unusual 4.30 layout from 1972 proved a hit but was said not to be very stable on tow.

The popular makes of the early 1970s had been Swift, Ace, A Line, Abbey, Sprite, Eccles, Europa, Fairholme and also Cavalier, whose simple profile offered users plenty of interior space. They also brought out interesting layouts such as the 440 GT, a 4.4m-long tourer with an L-shaped front lounge and rear end, an L-shaped kitchen with slide extending washroom and central dinette. It sold well and in 1973 came with under-floor insulation. It was also extended to 4.9m on a twin axle. The original 430 version in 1971 had been on a single axle.

By the late 1970s sales had picked up slightly but by 1979 a slump saw the number produced drop below 30,000. Manufacturers struggled, even Ci, which began to offload some of its foreign manufacturers. As it saw its market decline, Sam Alper saw exports slow and market share in the

ENJOY THE BEST OF BOTH WORLDS

CARAVAN *canal cruising*

THROUGH THE BEAUTIFUL YORKSHIRE DALES

(at approx. ½ the cost of conventional Cruiser Hire)

with YOUR OWN mobile caravan aboard

the UNIQUE self-drive "DALES-CRAFT" "TRAILER-SAILER"

(Patented)

THE LATEST AND GREATEST HOLIDAY HIRE TREND FOR THE '70s

View of a Trailer-Sailer with a Mobile Caravan housed in the safety well
TWO 3p STAMPS OR 5p P.O. for Illustrated Brochure with full details
and Map of Waterways served

To:— BRADFORD BOAT SERVICES LTD.

Yacht Station, Apperley Bridge

Bradford, Yorkshire   Telephone **Bradford 612827**

from motorway to cruiseway by "TRAILER - SAILER"

the easy way

It's the early 1970s, so fancy a caravan canal cruise? No? Nobody else did either and the idea was dropped.

UK decline. New models were brought in such as the Sprite Compact, a pop-top tourer that was launched in 1981 to success, although the build quality was not the best. Astral, which had developed new ranges covering all price sectors for 1979, had collapsed by the following year. Caravan dealers also felt the effects of the decline and small concerns shut down. The British Caravan Road Rally was to finish, but in the late 1970s Ci set up a tow-car competition that still stands and is now run by the Caravan and Motorhome Club, with another by the Camping and Caravanning Club.

The late 1970s had been tough, but caravanning still had an attraction as commercial sites were upgraded to make it more attractive. One novel idea was tried by Bradford Boat Services, who adapted a canal boat that could take a touring caravan. The idea was that you popped your caravan on the boat and had a canal cruise break. It was named the 'Trailer-Sailer', but it proved all too easy to fall into the canal while trying to walk around the caravan. Perhaps unsurprisingly, the idea sunk – if you will forgive the pun!

Memories

Edwin and Joyce Howson: We bought our first tourer, a 1981 ABI Monza 1000/Ford Escort 1.6, in 1986. We had some great holidays – this photo was taken near Holker Hall in Cumbria in 1988 (Joyce was pregnant with our daughter Alison!). It was a warm weekend if we remember right, with our then 3-year-old son Richard. We were with friends and had a great weekend.

Edwin and Joyce Howson, 1988.

The early 1980s saw depressed sales, with Ci going bust and then being saved and slimmed down. Thomson fell too, along with clubman makers Stirling and Royale, even though both these manufacturers had branched into making cheaper ranges. New construction methods and more standard equipment on tourers would stimulate new interest in caravanning, plus aerodynamics played a part. Eric Prue, a Ci dealer in Oxfordshire, designed and built Alpha Sport caravans (roughly 100 made) and they showed just how aerodynamic caravans could be. Prue set a world speed towing record at RAF Elvington in 1980 with an Aston Martin V8 Le Mans car at just short of 125mph! Sites had become better equipped with modern toilet facilities to attract more to caravanning. Mains electrics and 12V electrics saw gas lighting phased out from the mid-1980s and luxury models being equipped with mains sockets and battery chargers.

Eric Prue had ideas about aerodynamics with his speed-record Alpha 14 tourer in 1980.

The 1980s was the start of the twin-axle revolution with the advent of more 4×4 vehicles. You could take your tourer almost anywhere, no matter what size!

Above: Cosalt moved luxury brand Safari to Abbey's Grimsby works and produced a modern high-spec version. This is the first Safari XL44 out of the factory. (Courtesy Gary Wilkinson)

Left: The 1986 Swift factory with the lighter roofs extensions. This site is now a housing estate and the factory has moved to a 45-acre plot further down the road. (Swift Group)

The humble caravan loo was now a cassette design, but it wasn't fixed into the caravan. Carver Heating, with their SB1800 gas fire and double glazing, meant the caravan could be used even in colder months. This period was also to witness the popularity of the twin-axle caravan. With tow cars such as the Mitsubishi Shogun and Land Rover becoming seen as the ideal tow vehicle, the 4×4 revolution saw caravan manufacturers make bigger tourers and add more features. Thanks to the new lighter caravans a new band of caravan buyers saw sales rise in 1984. Swift began expanding, buying up land for factory extensions. Cosalt's Abbey did too and their offshoot luxury brand Safari got a makeover, dropping the traditional look for an ultra-modern profile and spec. ABI had remained strong in the downturn and launched new models to appeal to new caravanners.

The National Caravan Council's TV and radio 'Caravanning – get up and go' campaign in 1987 had a major impact on the popularity of the pastime.

Luxury maker Avondale, with their Perle and Leda ranges, also scored highly with twin-axle models that remained lightweight. At one point Bessacarr dropped all their single-axle models in favour of twins. The National Caravan Council also wanted to encourage more families into caravanning. The economy was booming and in

1986–87 all new models had a £40 tariff to help with a big marketing campaign. Radio ads and TV commercials were shown highlighting the freedom of caravanning; in fact, the campaign was named 'Caravanning – get up and go'. Cups and other items were printed with the slogan. ABI provided the caravans for the ads, which were stripped of their badges, of course!

This period saw many take to Scotland and Wales for holidays, and the Caravan and Motorhome Club opened more sites and upgraded existing ones to encourage new members. By this period two new manufacturers, Coachman and Vanroyce, had joined the now depleted ranks. Both quickly established themselves, while Swift had grown and Elddis under ABI also saw increased sales and developed new models. New car models such as the Vauxhall Cavalier proved excellent tow cars along with the Volvo brand. Caravanning was cool, although sales were never to reach the heights of pre-1973. Dealerships that had survived now got bigger but some, such as Gailey, collapsed.

The new breed of 1980s tourers from the likes of Fleetwood and the reborn Ci were attractive inside and out. Swift produced new aerodynamic models using glass-fibre moulds produced in their own factory. Even basic tourers came with double glazing and fridge plus a heater, with optional upgrades for hot water and showers. One big deal was the introduction of the Thetford cassette toilet fitted by ABI in their luxury Awards from 1989. This more civilised loo meant you went outside to a hatch and slid the full cassette out to dispose of waste.

With all the new innovations, it meant that there was more to go wrong and ideas were mooted for an official service schedule for tourers, which eventually won the day. By the middle to end of the 1980s, designs for tourers had come on in big leaps and set the way for the 1990s onwards. The 1970s had begun with a boom, with caravanning abroad becoming especially popular with UK owners, and this was a trend that would continue to the present day.

The early 1980s saw makers and dealerships go bust. Gailey had twenty-eight outlets and all of them would close apart from one.

The mid-1970s saw caravanners flock abroad with their vans thanks to improved ferry services, and this carried on into the 1980s.

Memories

David and Juliet Lomas: We have had several tourers over the years. This was our 1972 Sprite 400 in 1984. My daughter was only young here. We liked sites generally that were quiet. The Ford Granada proved an excellent tow car for the Sprite, although we later sold the Sprite for a Swift Danette, a larger and more comfortable tourer.

Juliet Lomas with her daughter in 1984.

5.

Caravanning Enters a New Era

The 1980s had ended on a high for the caravanner, with most sites now having mains pitches and room for awnings. The fact that more caravans had electrics fitted as standard meant that those without electrics fitted in their tourer felt left out of the modern caravanning world. But fear not because the caravan accessory market had the answer: the DIY fit-it-yourself mains kit! This provided you with the basics, but having heard of several caravanners fitting their own and tripping the site electrics, it was really better left to a qualified electrician!

By the 1990s sites had larger pitches for awnings and also had mains hook-ups. (Andrew Jenkinson Photography)

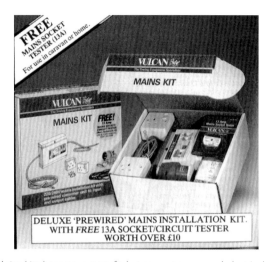

Mains kits became a retro fit, but some caravanners' electrical skills could be dubious.

By the late 1990s/early 2000s fridges were larger and more efficient. (Andrew Jenkinson Photography)

With electrics being fitted at the factory on tourers that were above entry level, there was no need for a charger unit. The on-board battery now powered the 12V lights in the caravan and the water pump too, and this was topped up by the mains charger when on site. The caravan fridge had now been developed to run on battery power (only when the car engine was on) as well as gas and mains electrics.

The heaters were by Carver, which had developed further units from the SB1250 and more powerful SB1800 in the 1970s. A blown system could be added, but wet central heating, i.e. Alde, was a still long way off as yet. However, the more luxury 2008 ranges would have Alde heating fitted as standard. The tow car of the year competition was still going strong, with Deanline and then ABI supplying the caravans.

The original Ci had begun the tow car of the year competition and by the 1990s it was firmly established.

In the early 1990s, there were still some 1980s accessories around, such as the 'Easylift' inflatable caravan jack, but sales were slow.

Reg Dean was a prolific manufacturer by 1981 because he had bought A Line – his old employer – from the receivers and renamed the company Deanline. Now in full control of his designs, he

Above: Launched in the 1980s, this easy jack lift didn't sell but could be found in caravan accessory shops into the '90s.

Right: Swift's investment in style and aerodynamics gave their tourers the edge. The 1992 Swift Alouette was a good example of this.

could create some new tourers such as the twin-axle luxury Link that came with a microwave and an on-board generator! He also kept his Ramblers. By 1985 he had sold his company to ABI, where he stayed until it went out of business in 1997.

With even the most expensive tourers you were lucky to get three mains sockets – but the whole caravanning way of life was changing. The cheap caravan had all but gone

Cosalt sold the Abbey brands to Swift in the early 1990s and the company further developed ranges such as the Abbey Iona. (Andrew Jenkinson Photography)

but the touring caravan was becoming a more sophisticated vehicle. The 1990s would see Swift gain in the tourer market share; they had bought clubman manufacturer Cotswold Caravans and moved production from Grimsby to Cottingham. However, the new arrangement was not to be a success and the Cotswold name had gone by the early 1990s. In 1993, Cosalt sold its Abbey, Safari and Piper names to Swift, who again moved production to Cottingham and grew the brands over the years.

Swift would also acquire Sprite Leisure, which had been founded after the reborn Ci of the 1980s got into trouble again in the early '90s as a general slump in sales gave the industry a hard time. A buyout resulted in the company being

Swift's Sprite Excel range. The first of the Swift-built Sprites did not go down well in 1997. Until 2005 they were only built for export.

renamed Sprite Leisure, making Sprite, Eccles and Europa. Swift closed their Newmarket plant and moved the brands to Yorkshire. Bessacarr, the luxury brand of twin-axle tourers that had done so well in the 1980s, was to also be bought from its parent company Arnold Lever Group by Swift.

Swift were now only second in size and market share to ABI, which had become a public limited company in 1990 and had also sold its Elddis division off. ABI had become a major force with its tourers, holiday homes and Auto Trail motorhomes, along with Vanroyce, the luxury brand it had bought out. But the company was stockpiling its output and went out of business in 1997. Its motorhome division and Vanroyce, also built at the Auto Trail factory, was sold to Trigano. In 1998, ABI re-formed with a new buyer as ABI UK and traded for several years with limited success. By 2001, ABI was the subject of a management buyout and the tourer ranges Award, Monza, Ace, Target and Jubilee were all sold to Swift, with ABI concentrating on holiday caravans.

Coachman's VIP luxury range had lots of spec and became a top seller. This is a 1997 interior.

Adria have imported into UK since 1971. They offer UK buyers an alternative to home-built models, including this Action compact two-berth. (Andrew Jenkinson Photography)

Castleton, the small Dorset maker, folded in 1995, while a new company, Vanmaster (no connection to the DIY shells), began making luxury tourers. Elddis became the Explorer Group and gradually bought out firms such as Buccaneer, Compass and Coachman, a newer maker of quality tourers that was established in 1986–87. Coachman would eventually buy themselves out of Elddis to become independent again, but by 2020, they had been bought by Kabe, the Swedish maker. Imported tourers had done quite well in the late 1980s, with Adria making inroads in the UK market with a good selection of dealerships. Hobby and Tabbert also sold into the UK but in smaller numbers.

The Earls Court show was now becoming a shadow of its former self, with the February Boat and Caravan Show taking the main footfall. The number of visitors dropped from 160,000-plus

Earls Court, 1997. It was the main venue for all things caravan, but the show was to end in the mid-2000s.

The Birmingham show took over from Earls Court in October 2006, with the spring show held in February. (Andrew Jenkinson Photography)

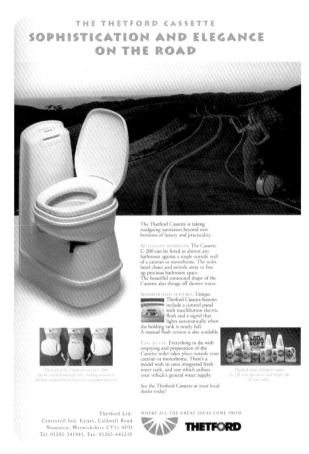

*The Thetford cassette toilet was hygienic and would eventually
come with electric flush. This was the first swivel model manual
flush, ideal for small washrooms in tourers.*

to 40,000, and by 2005 it had gone, replaced by a new main show at the NEC in October. It was all part of the ever-changing world of the UK caravan industry.

The cassette toilet by Thetford had been a game changer for loo facilities in caravans. In the early 1990s, Thetford introduced the swivel unit with electric flush, a design that proved ideal for end washroom layouts. The end washroom idea has been around since the 1920s but it became a top seller in the 1990s in both two- and four-berth layouts and took over the traditional end kitchen design in popularity.

ABI UK had tried to catch the public's imagination with several trend-setting designs, such as using pastel colours in their Papillion range, while they also showed off the ABI Lilac Sprinter redesigned exterior and interior by designer Linda Barker, but there was no public uptake of the new look. The 2000s were to see Fleetwood and Avondale go out of business.

An Avondale Osprey. These were smart-looking tourers, light and well specified. Production ended in late 2008. (Andrew Jenkinson Photography)

Dealer specials would gain more popularity from the mid-2000s. This is a Sprite special for one-time dealership Barrons Great Outdoors (named Firebrand). (Andrew Jenkinson Photography)

Designer Linda Baker looks out from her Lilac ABI UK Sprinter at Earls Court in 1997. The idea was not put into production.

Clockwise from right: Bailey's Ranger from 1996 was a huge success, selling well until 2010. It offered spec, light weight and value.

Lunar's Quasar range was light and well equipped. (Andrew Jenkinson Photography)

By 2005 Bailey had gained a large share of the market with Ranger, Pageant Senator and Discovery. Pictured is the 2005 Series 5 Ranger 460/4. (Andrew Jenkinson Photography)

The 1980s had seen what was termed a 'dealer special', which consisted of a standard tourer range with added specifications but costing less than if the buyer had bought the standard model and added to it. By the late 1990s and into the 2000s, the dealer special had become a popular choice, with all manufacturers producing a range for several dealers and often using old caravan names from the past. The biggest makers may have been Swift and Elddis but by the mid-'90s Bristol-based Bailey would launch a range of lightweight, well-equipped tourers at below £10,000, naming them Rangers. The upshot was that Rangers were very well received. Bailey played on this format, with their Pageants and Senators adding spec yet offering incredible value, and they sold extremely well. By 2010, Bailey chose a new direction with Alu-Tech construction, changing the ranges and the company format.

By the early 2000s Bailey would be one of the top-selling brands in the UK. They were a formidable force in the market, although companies such as Lunar would also produce good value, lightweight models such as the Clubmans and Quasar. The caravan market saw customers wanting more spec and, with the addition of microwaves, TV aerials, fridges, ovens, showers, blown air and wet central-heating systems, the weight of tourers had gone up, although manufacturers were trying to keep it down. Awnings had become the must-have accessory, and the BBQ would become another essential for the caravanner.

TV aerials were mostly fitted as standard. Status have basically cornered the market with their excellent products. (Andrew Jenkinson Photography)

Memories

Garry and Marylyn Battern: I have caravanned for years and became a member of the Sprite Owners' Club years ago. I love Sprite and what they stand for: value. This photo is me in 1992 with my daughter Angela with my Sprite Alpine C. Angela now has her own Sprite and me and Marylyn caravan whenever we can.

Garry Battern and his daughter Angela around 1992.
(Garry Battern)

The towing of tourers had always been a problem for some wanting to go caravanning, but with new systems to help stability, such as the AKS hitch stabiliser, BPW chassis or ATC, users gained more confidence while towing. The development of the caravan motor mover over the years has also meant that the days of pushing a caravan onto its pitch or up the drive are over, with it all being done remotely with little effort.

With more sites opening up all year, the caravan has reinforced its value-for-money tag, enabling the owner to get more use from their investment. Winter caravanning, especially through Christmas and New Year, would gain more popularity as tourers were well insulated and equipped with efficient heating systems.

Caravanning was becoming a lifestyle as the models became more expensive, but again the spec and construction improved to offset these costs. The sunroof idea in tourers had been around for some years (Avondale's Leda range in the early 1980s had one), but it

The Al-Ko AKS hitch stabiliser improves towing stability and is pretty much standard fit now. (Andrew Jenkinson Photography)

Handling tourers was always a difficult job. The invention of the mover made moving so much easier, with several makes now on the market. (Andrew Jenkinson Photography)

Caravanning all year round has become more common. (Andrew Jenkinson Photography)

would be Swift and Coachman that would help set a trend in 2010–11. The touring caravan celebrated its 100th year in 2019. How things have changed, such as the fact that caravan hire was once so popular but is virtually unheard of now.

The motorhome and campervan may offer a different style of freedom to the touring caravan but through all its ups and downs the latter has remained popular as ever. With the advent of the electric car, the touring caravan will need to

Sam Alper at home in 2000. He shaped the industry and design in many ways, being shrewd and forward thinking. (Andrew Jenkinson Photography)

The Gobur Carousel fold-up tourer from 2009. These Norfolk-built caravans served a niche market sector. (Andrew Jenkinson Photography)

Swift's Sprite range is a best seller. This is the 2022 new model Sprite Compact (Compact was a name last used on a 1981 Sprite pop-top). (Andrew Jenkinson Photography)

adapt, or maybe the electric car will need to be designed more with towing in mind. The 8ft-wide caravan has become successful as families want more internal space. Fixed-bed designs took off in the 2000s, along with fixed bunk beds. Such changes to layouts have to be made to cater for changing needs and to keep caravanning as appealing as possible.

Throughout all the decades, the touring caravan has remained a firm favourite with families and couples alike. Sam Alper must be credited as the man who gave caravanning to the working classes with his value Sprites. The time and effort he took in promoting caravanning on endurance runs and in setting speed-towing records certainly put caravans in front of many who would not have previously considered owning one.

The market for the folding caravan that we saw in the early days dried up and UK brand Carousel ceased production after nearly forty years.

Left: Sprite Compact interior, a far cry from Sam Alper's early 1950s Sprites! (Andrew Jenkinson Photography)

Elddis, begun by the Cook family as a small concern in 1964, is now a large operation owned by the Hymer Group. These are new 2022 models lined up for a trade show.

The last few years has seen tourers from Elddis and associate brands offer new levels of comfort and specification. The luxury Buccaneers aren't hand built like they used to be but they still have a heritage behind them that makes these tourers popular, despite costing nearly £40,000! At Swift, Peter Smith, the son of founder Ken Smith, has seen his father's company grow to a large concern but only through investment in design and marketing. Swift would make its Sprite brand the best-selling in the UK, offering Alperson's original concept of value for money. The Eccles name that had been the foundation stone of the touring caravan was dropped by Swift after its 100th year in 2019, although hopefully the company will bring it back. Sadly, Lunar ceased production in 2019, in what would have been their fiftieth year.

Coachman, founded by Jim Hibbs who sadly passed away in 2018, has prospered under his son Elliot's guidance, with its latest models such as the VIP and Laser. In 2020, Kabe of Sweden purchased Coachman, securing the brand's future. Adria still retains its share of the UK market, now being owned by Trigano, while Elddis is owned by Hymer. So after more than a century of towing, in many ways the touring caravan still retains its roots from the days when caravanning was still very much in its infancy.

Changes have taken place, with the Caravan Club being renamed the Caravan and Motorhome Club, while exports are only a fraction of what they once were. There are few caravan manufacturers now left in the UK, and out of those that are, only Swift and Bailey remain in UK ownership. However, the touring caravan retains its appeal and without many of the names mentioned in this book it would not be as popular as it is today, not just in the UK but in Europe too.

Memories

Andy Craven: My parents' Land Rover long wheel base and their 1969 Sprite Musketeer on a night stop-over by Loch nan Uamh viaduct in 1985 with a BR train coming through. We used to go to Scotland and the Highlands a lot for our summer holidays – great memories.

Andy Craven in 1985, showing his parents' Land Rover and Sprite.

If you enjoyed this title from The History Press

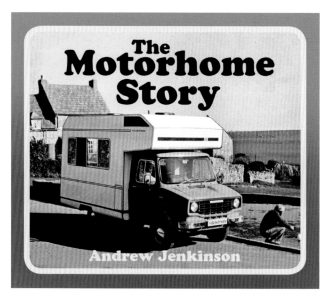

978 0 7509 9490 3

The destination for history
www.thehistorypress.co.uk